DEAD GORGE
Fantastic Outfits from History

Let's Travel Back in Time!
History is all about the past. Now some people think the past is dead and buried. It happened so long ago, it must be dead dull. Right? Wrong! The past never really goes away. In fact, it's all around us. We can read about it in books. We can see it in old pictures. We can visit old places and imagine what they were like many years ago. It's like travelling back in time. Now that's dead interesting – isn't it?

Contents

Have you ever wondered what wacky outfits people in the past used to wear? Well, this is the place to find out! Imagine a time before jeans and T-shirts. A time before zips and buttons. How did people cope? What did they wear? And most importantly of all, did they look dead gorgeous?

Chapter 1
Dress to Impress   4
Surprising facts about looking good in the past.

Chapter 2
Extremely Cool Eygptians   8
How to cope with the heat *and* look cool.

Chapter 3
Greeks and Romans – All Wrapped Up   12
Getting to grips with the 'baggy' look.

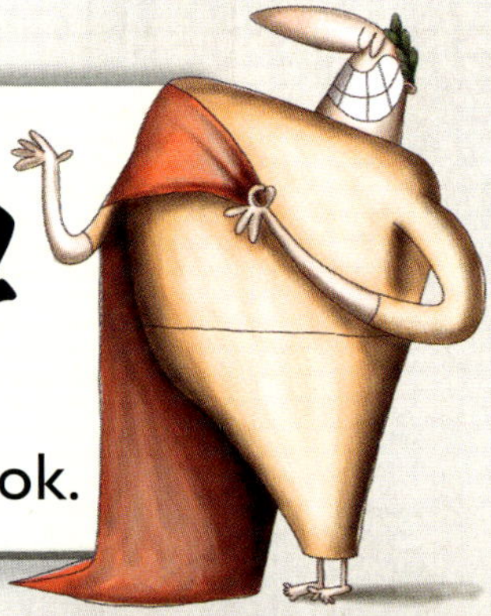

Chapter 4
Tight Fits from France   16
Squeezing into the latest fashions.

Chapter 5
Over-the-Top Tudors   20
Was BIG really better?

Chapter 6
Sensible Victorians   24
See how fashion was made much easier.

Chapter 7
Well, Were You Impressed?   28
What clothes from the past would *you* like to wear?

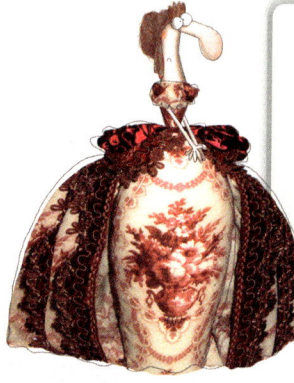

Timeline   30

Glossary and Index   32

Chapter 1
Dress to Impress

It takes money to look this good!

A lot of people today like to look dead gorgeous. So did people in the past. You'll soon see what outfits they wore. But first, here are some facts that might surprise you about fashion in history ...

Who Cares About Fashion?

You may think that fashion is just for girls. But in history, both men and women wanted to look gorgeous. They went out of their way to do this and wore some truly eye-popping outfits.

You look dead gorgeous, darling.

You too, my dear.

Expensive Fashions

Not all men and women could wear gorgeous clothes like the ones in this book. Only rich people could really afford to buy them. They paid a **tailor** or a **dressmaker** to make their clothes by hand.

Most people in history owned very few clothes. Usually they had to make their clothes themselves. They used rough, cheap **fabrics** and had to wear them until they fell to bits.

Dressing Up Like Mum and Dad

In the past, it wasn't easy to tell a very young boy from a very young girl. Why not? Because they wore clothes that looked exactly the same.

Then, as they got older, children wore smaller versions of grown-ups' clothes. It was dead easy to see who came from a rich family and who didn't. Poorer children had rough, homemade clothes just like their parents. Rich children had fine clothes just like *their* parents, too.

Different Times in History

Before we start looking at old outfits, let's get a few words clear:

- Stuff that happened a very long time ago is called **Ancient History**.
- Stuff that happened quite recently is called **Modern History**.
- The time in between is called the Middle Ages – and stuff that happened in the Middle Ages is called **Medieval History**.

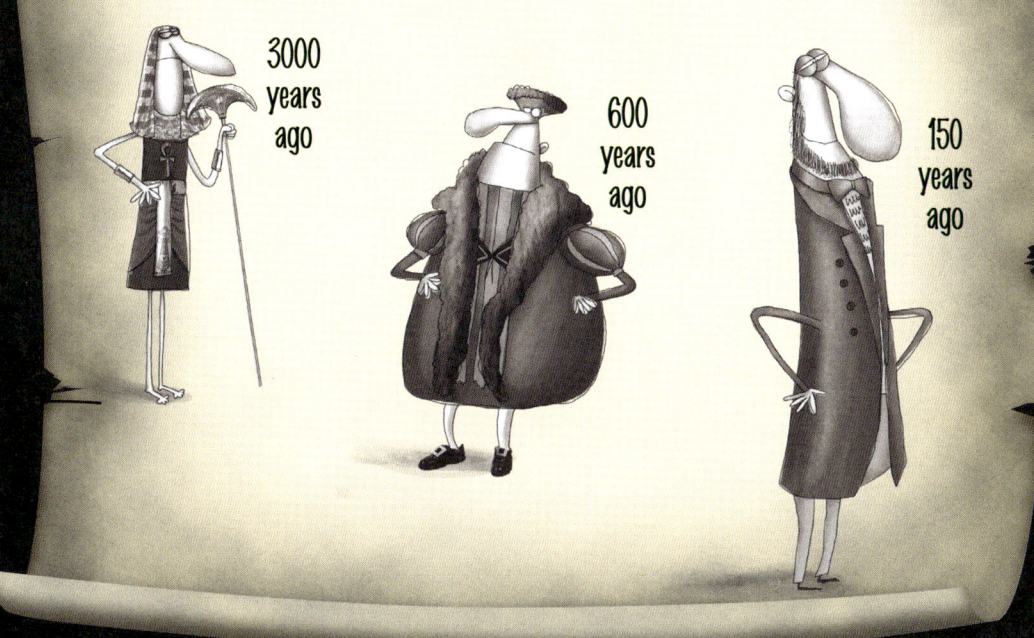

3000 years ago

600 years ago

150 years ago

Got all that? Great! Fasten your seat-belts. We'll travel right back to ancient times first.

Chapter 2
Extremely Cool Egyptians

Let's chill!

Time: Three to four thousand years ago.
Place: Ancient Egypt in North Africa

Egyptian people didn't just want to look cool. It was very hot in Africa so they needed to feel cool too. They found some strange ways of doing this!

We slaves have no trouble keeping cool. We don't wear any clothes at all!

Slaves Only

Who is who?

Rich Egyptian men liked to look as good as their wives. In fact they often looked quite similar!

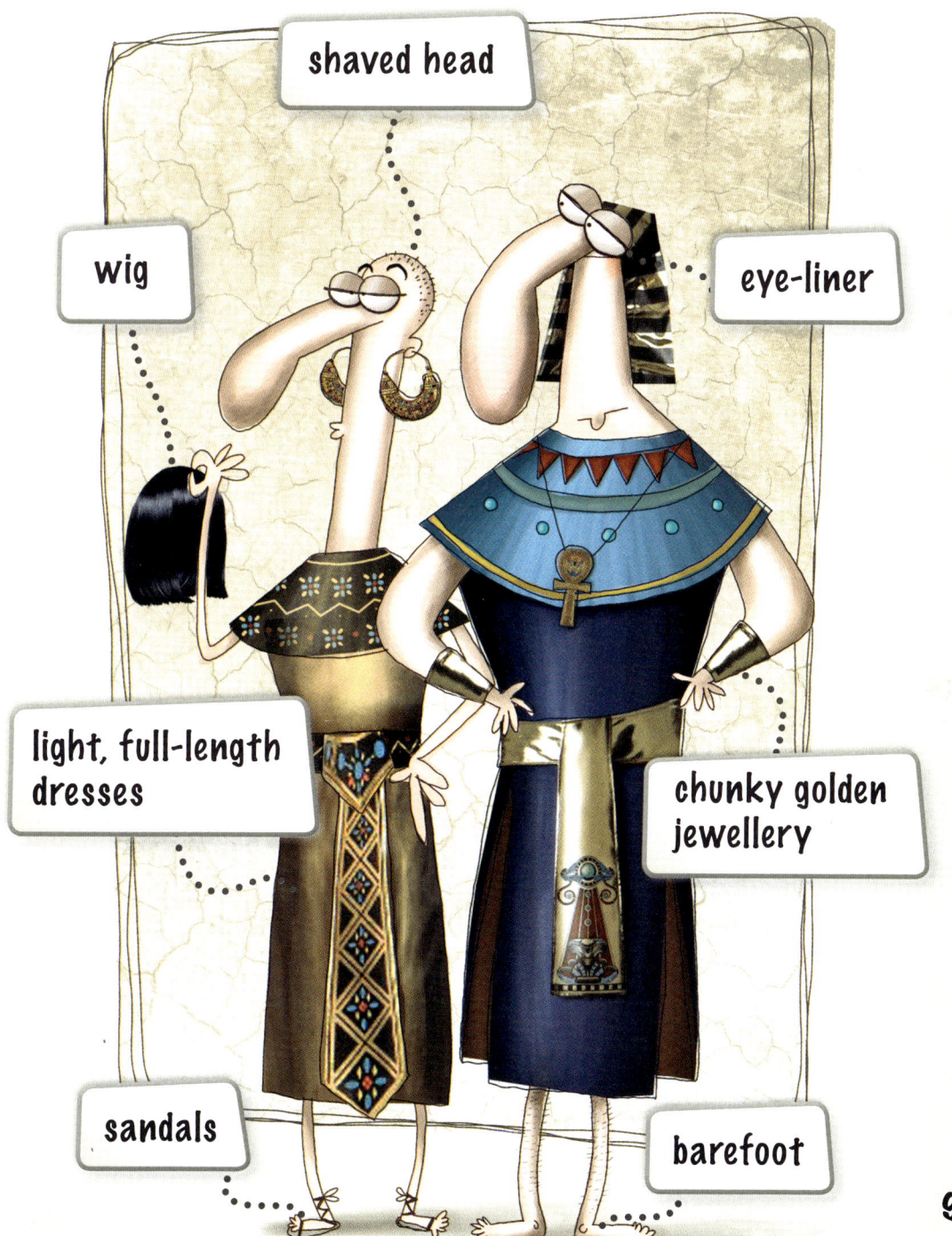

This Egyptian man and his wife were dead fashionable about 3350 years ago.

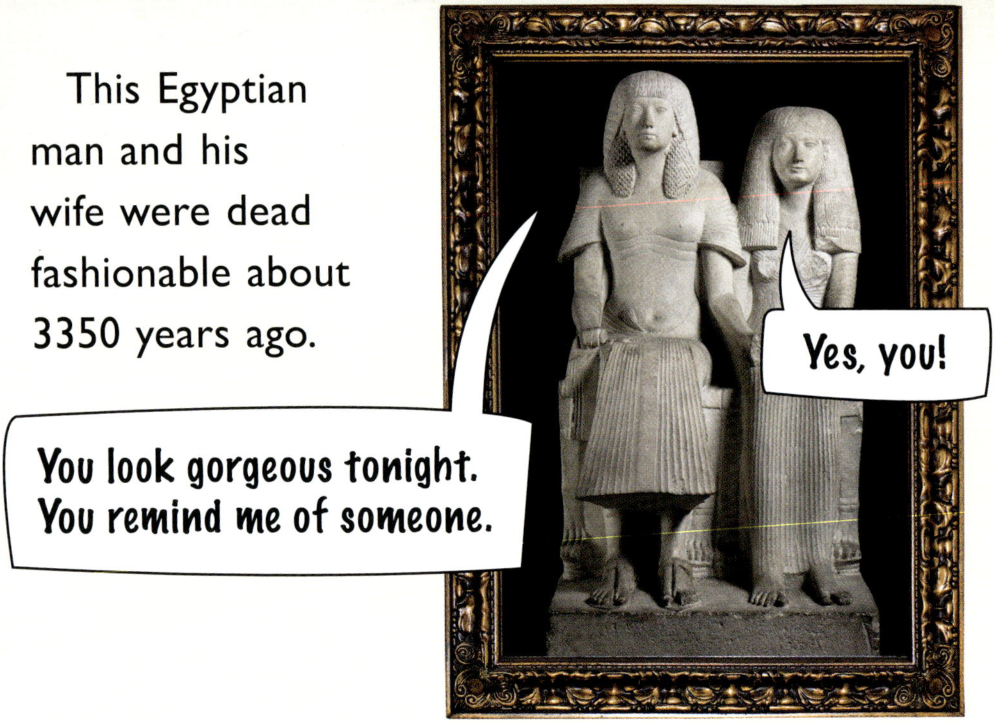

Yes, you!

You look gorgeous tonight. You remind me of someone.

Clothes Fit for a King

Fashionable Egyptians wore clothes made of cotton or linen. Egypt's kings, called pharaohs, wore clothes made with gold thread. Poorer people had to make do with clothes made out of dried **reeds!**

You have to *dry* the reeds first!

Cool Hair

Fashionable Egyptians also wore wigs which were quite hot. So, how could they look cool *and* keep a cool head?

Feel good! Smell Great! Look Gorgeous!

Next time you are hot, cool down with a scented wax cone. Just pop it on top of your wig. Then relax as it melts! Your head and shoulders will be bathed in lovely perfume! Your skin will glow!

"Hmm. This wax works!"

Today, fashions seem to change every week. In ancient times, new styles came along much less often. Let's jump ahead to see how the Ancient Greeks and Romans did things …

Chapter 3
Greeks and Romans – All Wrapped Up

Time: *Two to three thousand years ago.*
Place: *Ancient Greece and Rome in Southern Europe*

Ancient Greeks and Romans wore heavier clothes than Ancient Egyptians. They loved to wrap themselves up in big, loose **garments**. And both men and women wanted to be dead gorgeous!

This looks like a Greek woman getting ready to go out. It's not, it's a man. Greek men spent *lots* of time getting ready to go out.

Rich Greek women didn't actually go out much. They were supposed to be busy running the home and bringing up children. But that didn't stop rich women dressing up, even if no one got to see them!

Long Chitons and Tricky Togas

Greek men and women draped themselves in chitons (say: *sheetons*). A chiton had so much material in it, you could:

- wear it loose and just let it hang
- use a belt to pull it in at the waist
- use its folds to make pretend sleeves
- use a fold to form a hood!

In Rome, a little later than in Greece, rich women wore elegant long robes and colourful shawls. The men wore togas (say: *toe-gers*). Togas were like big, oval-shaped blankets and were tricky to put on.

PUT YOUR TOGA ON IN 4 EASY STEPS

1. Put one end over your left shoulder.

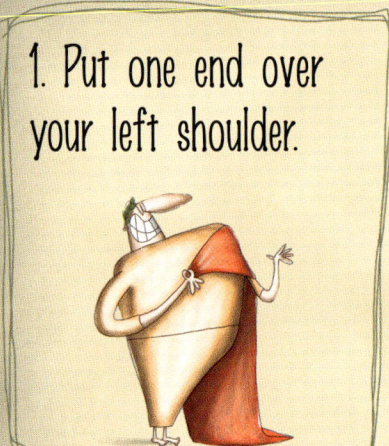

2. Bring the other end under your right arm.

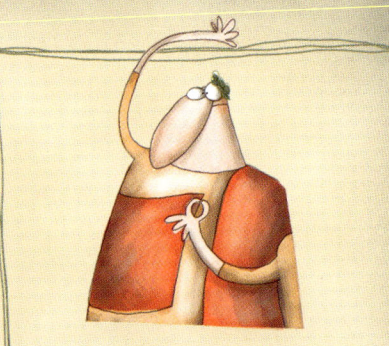

3. Put the right end over your left shoulder too.

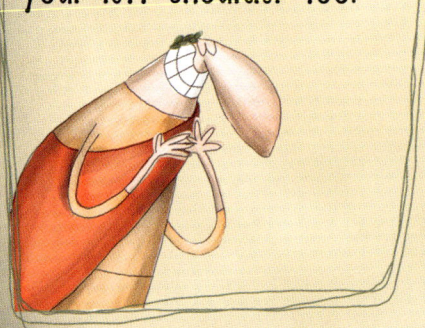

4. Tuck the middle into the belt of your tunic.

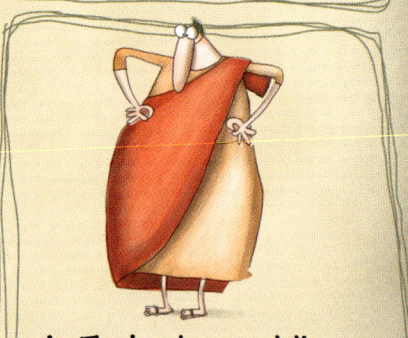

Now you look great and are ready to go!

Toga Rules

There were strict rules about the colours togas could be. For example, important men had a purple border on their togas. The size of your toga also showed how important you were. Some togas were massive – 5.49m long and 3.51m wide!

I'm in here somewhere – and I'm *very* important!

The Ancient Greeks and Romans loved loose clothes. But a thousand years later, the baggy look was truly over …

Chapter 4
Tight Fits from France

Time: The Middle Ages, about 600 years ago.
Place: France and elsewhere in Western Europe

By the 1400s, Europe's richest people had gone clothes crazy! New styles spread from country to country and fashion was all about showing off!

Medieval Fashion Tips

- Don't hide yourself in baggy clothes.
- Show your slender arms, girls!
- Show your shapely legs, guys!
- Think of the fabrics you can wear — velvets, silks and furs in all the colours of the rainbow!
- Greeks and Romans are ancient history.
- Move with the times — GET MEDIEVAL!

Is my hat big enough?

Tight Fits

Rich medieval women loved showing off their figures. They wore dresses with narrow waists and tight sleeves. They wore thick velvet gowns to keep out winter chills.

Men wore decorated tunics called doublets (say: *dub-lets*). On their legs they wore tight leggings called hose. There wasn't any room for pockets so they had purses on their belts instead.

Extraordinary Hats and Shoes

But not *all* the clothes were figure-hugging. When it came to medieval heads and feet, BIG was BEAUTIFUL!

This old painting shows a medieval couple getting married. They clearly think they look dead gorgeous.

Walk this way.

I can't. Someone's standing on my dress!

Look at the lady's big hat. These hats could be as big as 1.2 m high. That's almost as tall as the lady underneath!

Look at the man's shoes. Men in medieval Europe loved long, pointy shoes. The longer the shoes, the better. In England, a law said rich people could wear shoes up to 61cm long! Ordinary people were not supposed to wear shoes longer than 15cm.

Not everyone thought that big was better. In fact, one **bishop** thought that using so much fabric in just one dress was very wasteful indeed.

Other medieval people also thought clothes had become *too* crazy. But as time passed, clothes didn't get more sensible. In fact they went right over the top ...

Chapter 5
Over-the-Top Tudors

> Does my neck look big in this?

Time: The Tudor period, 400–500 years ago.
Place: England and elsewhere in Europe

Rich Tudor people dressed to make a BIG impression. The bigger the clothes, the better. But that meant they wore some very strange outfits.

Take a look at this. It's made of hoops of **whalebone** sewn into fabric. What do you think it is?

> A bell? An upside-down flowerpot?

It is actually called a farthingale. Tudor ladies wore them under their dresses. Why? To make their skirts really wide.

Big is Best

It wasn't just the women who thought that big was beautiful. A new fashion from Spain thrilled Tudor men. The ruff was a fancy collar. It was so big and stiff, you sometimes needed wires to hold it up!

Tudor Troubles
Tell Auntie Anne all your woes.

Hungry in Harrogate: I love wearing Spanish ruffs. But my ruff is so wide I'm finding it hard to get food into my mouth. I'm afraid I'll starve to death! What can I do?

Auntie Anne: My dear man, all you need is a long-handled spoon!

Important Tudor people paid a lot of money for stiff, uncomfortable clothes – but somehow they still managed to dance …

Does my bottom look big in this farthingale? I hope so!

You can also see that they wore big padded sleeves. Sometimes they had slashes in their clothes too. This was to show off *more* clothing underneath.

Big really was best in Tudor times. But there weren't any style magazines back then. So how did rich people know what was in fashion?

Fashionable Dolls

Tudor ladies really did have dolls to show them the latest fashions. Every detail of the dress on the doll was correct. The dressmaker just copied what the doll was wearing.

The Tudors knew how to catch the eye with their big fashions. But did clothes *go on* getting bigger? Did men go on looking as flashy as women?

Chapter 6
Sensible Victorians

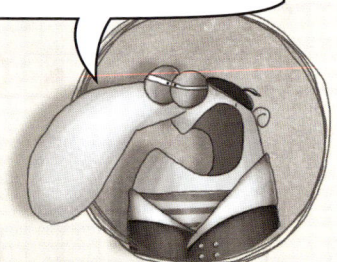

Sensible doesn't always mean good!

Time: About 150 years ago.
Place: Britain, Europe and the USA

In the mid-1800s, fashions finally got a bit more sensible. There were also big changes in how clothes were made and bought.

The queen who ruled Britain at the time was called Victoria. We now call the people who lived then 'Victorians'. Rich Victorian men and women weren't as flashy as the Tudors. They still wanted to look dead gorgeous, but in less crazy ways.

I'm very glad we don't have to wear clothes like that!

Ladies still liked to show off their tiny waists. But their waists weren't always quite as tiny as they seemed. They wore very tight, stiff garments under their clothes, called corsets, to make their waists really small.

You look gorgeous.

I know. But I can't breathe out.

Men wore smart, sensible coats. They also wore trousers – usually in quite dark colours. When bicycles were invented, ladies got their own type of trousers called bloomers. They couldn't go riding bikes in great big dresses!

All Change in the Fashion World

Not all Victorian outfits were still made by hand. Special machines were used to make different fabrics. Then sewing machines were invented. Clothes could now be made much faster. But an even bigger change was on the way …

Ready-Made Clothes

Around 1860, the first **fashion houses** opened. These were places where rich people could buy new outfits. Top **designers** created the clothes there – so they cost top prices!

7th February 1861

My dear,

Have you heard of the latest thing? You no longer need to tell a dressmaker what clothes to make. Now you go to a fashion house and simply pick a dress that has already been made! The Queen shops at these places too!

Best wishes,
Lady Dale

She used to order just one dress at a time!

But you didn't need a queen's riches to buy stylish clothes. Less wealthy Victorian men and women shopped at **department stores**. They could buy copies of what the rich people were wearing for much less money.

For the first time ever, people could also buy outfits made just for children. These outfits were still based on what the adults wore. Little sailor suits for boys were very popular.

We wait thousands of years for our own clothes. Then they make us look like *sailors*!

By the time Queen Victoria died in 1901, it was becoming easier and cheaper for lots of people to buy the latest fashions. You didn't have to be dead rich to be dead gorgeous any more!

Chapter 7
Well, Were You Impressed?

So now you've seen just some of the ways people used to dress to impress in the past. Would *you* like to wear one of these eye-popping outfits?

Remember that if you had lived before 1900, you would have worn only natural fabrics like wool, silk or cotton. There were also no zips or safety pins, and no electric irons to iron your clothes!

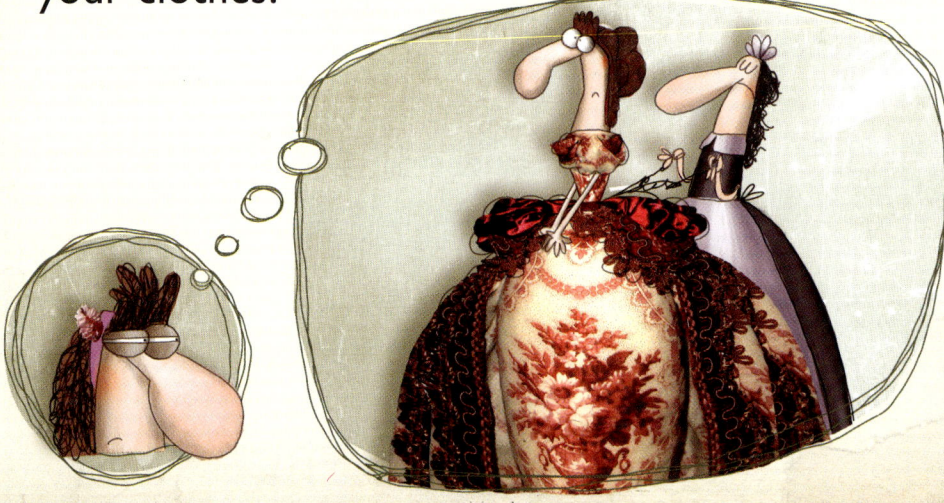

Last of all, remember this: only a tiny number of men, women and children ever got to look dead gorgeous. Most people's clothes were old, smelly and uncomfortable. That wasn't much fun at all!

So, maybe the clothes you are wearing now suit you better. But you could still wear an eye-popping outfit from the past to a fancy dress party!

Timeline

Here are some of the fashions featured in this book with the dates they were popular:

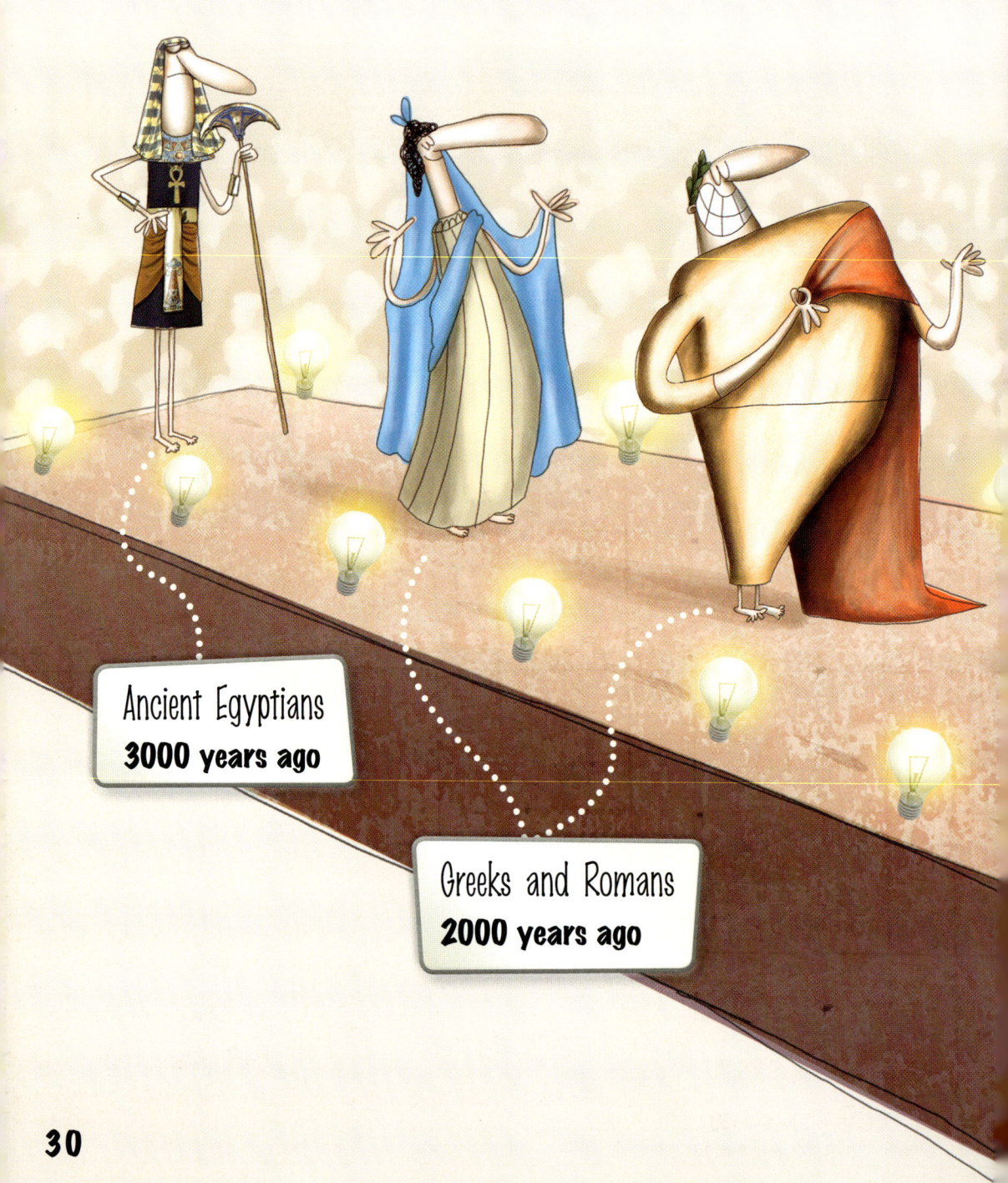

Ancient Egyptians
3000 years ago

Greeks and Romans
2000 years ago

Glossary

bishop: important person in the Christian Church

department stores: large shops with separate areas, each selling a certain type of thing

designers: people who plan how clothes should look

dressmaker: someone who makes clothes for women

fabrics: materials used to make clothes

fashion houses: businesses that design, make and sell clothes

garments: items of clothing

reeds: tall grasses that grow in marshy places

tailor: someone who makes clothes

whalebone: piece of bone from a whale used to make clothes stiff

Index

bloomers 25
children 6, 27
chitons 13
corsets 25
designers 26
dolls 23
doublets 17
dressmakers 5, 23
Egyptians 8–11
fabrics 5, 10, 16, 28
farthingales 20
fashion houses 26
Greeks 12–13
hats 18
Middle Ages 16–19
poor people 6, 10
Romans 12, 14–15
ruffs 21
sewing machines 25
shoes 9, 18–19
slaves 8
tailors 5
togas 14–15
Tudor people 20–23
Victorians 24–27
wigs 9, 11